T0197393

AatmaYOG

A complete beginner's guide to self-heal emotions, mind, body and soul

By Garima Kapani

Balboa Press books may be ordered through booksellers or by contacting:

Balboa Press
A Division of Hay House
1663 Liberty Drive
Bloomington, IN 47403
www.balboapress.com
844-682-1282

ISBN: 978-1-9822-7788-8 (sc)
ISBN: 978-1-9822-7787-1 (e)

Print information available on the last page.

Balboa Press rev. date: 06/23/2022

BALBOA.PRESS
A DIVISION OF HAY HOUSE

Contents

Introduction

In order to attain peace of mind, we must understand that there is a voice within us that always guides us and can be relied upon. Alignment of the heart and mind creates peace. It is attained by listening to the heart and processing the information through the mind and not vice-versa. Peace is not something that is served to us because we wish or ask for it, it is in fact something that we make and spread, something that we can be and something that we radiate and attract. Peace is a lifestyle that we have the power to manifest, a habit that we form consciously through healing our emotions, mind, body and soul.

Aatmayog or oneness of the soul, brings together various spiritual paths integrated to form a healing technique that have proven to heal various aspects of human life.
I invite you to begin this journey with me.

Acknowledgement

A spiritual path is a long journey which is not always comforting. Throughout this journey, we meet people and create experiences that lead to self-discovery and a new way of life. Every being that we come across in life, from family to friends, from coworkers to acquaintances, every interaction we encounter, plays a role in the story of our life and becomes a part of our growth.

I am grateful to have found teachers that have gone above and beyond to transform me into the spiritual being that I am, who is constantly striving to attain knowledge and wisdom.

I would especially like to thank my teacher and Magister Cosmo Energy Healer Roby Tata, from Los Angeles, California who not only helped me heal from years of abuse and trauma through Cosmo healing but also taught me how to deal with emotions in a healthy way.

I would also like to thank my yoga, kundali activation (the coiled energy that rests at the base of the spine. When awakened and released in an individual, it brings great knowledge, wisdom and spiritual powers) and mudra guru Sri Suresh Aggarwal from New Delhi, India, who, with his own awakened kundali, empowered me to gain his knowledge and spread it through this book.

Lastly, I would like to express gratitude towards my mother, a Certified Master Cosmo Healer and an EFT practitioner, Archana Kapani, who has been my teacher and guide throughout my life. Without her support, my knowledge and this book was not possible.

I am grateful to my readers and students who keep faith in Aatmayog. It is with your support and belief that Aatmayog, Inc. is able to reach and help those who are open to holistic healing.

Preface

Spirituality is a door that is once open, we see various roads that are to be discovered. It can be confusing to determine, where to begin. In five years post my spiritual awakening, I took several of these paths to not just discover but heal myself.

In the world that we live in, we face innumerable emotional, physical and worldly challenges to survive. With the depression rate increasing more than ever, it is vital for each individual who is awakened, to help as many as possible fight their demons and pull out of darkness.

As an abuse survivor who has not only fought depression but have also created a blissful life for myself and my children, I consider my knowledge to be my responsibility to make it easier for those who aspire to take the spiritual path of self-discovery and the powers within, an easier journey through 'Aatmayog'- a healing journey of emotions, mind, body and soul to awaken the hidden powers of a spiritual being. 'Aatmayog', the oneness of soul, can be experienced through practicing the exercises provided in each chapter of this book or by attending Aatmayog retreats, classes and workshops. For more information, visit www.aatmayog.co.

Disclosure: The level of healing that an individual experiences is different for everyone. It is based on the underlying cause and its intensity, the type and number of sessions attended and personal dedication to follow the program. Although the program is designed so that every individual that practices it, feels a positive difference, everyone experiences its results differently.

Power of Acceptance

The first step towards healing any aspect of our being is, awareness. It is the initial realization that something needs to shift within us that puts us on a path of learning how to let go of ego and acknowledge the need to unlearn the beliefs that we were conditioned to create subconsciously as children or the beliefs that we have carried through past lives unconsciously with our soul. Accepting that which is unfamiliar can be scary, even if it looks appealing on the surface, stepping into an unknown territory takes courage. Understanding that by humbling down and facing our deepest fears and challenges, we will liberate ourselves, takes strength. It is no different than stepping into a dark tunnel alone, not knowing what is inside and where it will lead to, but taking the leap of faith just because there is an inner knowing which we call intuition that tells us that we have reached the phase of life where our shell that we have created to protect ourself from the unknown, must shed. That is when we begin to test the waters and answer the inner call that we must take to see the light at the end of the tunnel. This is what is called a spiritual awakening.

It is hard to admit that the difficult experiences of life are vital to attain wisdom that constructs the foundation of spirituality. We can choose to look at such experiences negatively or recognize them as opportunities to grow. When an unpleasant experience triggers an unaware human, they react through expressing feelings of anger, envy, hatred, etc. through their words or actions. An awakened human recognizes their emotion or reaction and its consequences and is able to make a mindful decision to not react but accept and heal themselves and the situation to the best of their ability. To understand this better, if we translate literally, the Sanskrit term for anger is 'Kamanuja' which means 'younger brother of desire.' Where an unaware human gets angry or reacts in defense when facing someone's anger, an awakened human understands that this reaction stems from a deep, unmet desire. This allows one to see the other person or oneself with humility and a greater understanding and provides the calmness one needs to resolve the deep rooted issue with patience instead of reacting irrationally.

It is through the hardships and difficult experiences of life that we question, how and why things are affecting us and those associated to us and what could be done differently to attain the desired outcome. Until we reach this stage, we experience similar patterns in our life, one after the other, unknowingly learning our life's lessons that our soul has come to this earth for. After all, why would one spend time to analyze and reason with a perfect life where no mistakes are ever made? Spiritual awakening challenges everything that we have ever known to be true and our mindset suddenly shifts to feel that our uniqueness is meant to drive our life's force to a bigger purpose and a deeper understanding of where we should be directing our energy. We then realize that there is more than just a physical body and there is something beyond the soul as we know it. A true spiritual awakening does not require leaving one's household and the life one has created or, people and responsibilities that one is committed to. It is in fact, embracing all that you have, and making the best of it.

Our brain is designed to feel comfort in what is familiar, even if its unpleasant or self-sabotaging. A lot of times people remain in abusive cycles because that is how they know life and that is what they attract with their unhealed energy. Some people tend to subconsciously start believing that happiness is not for them or in some cases, they doubt the intentions of those who make an effort to make them happy. Instead of welcoming it, they shut down, create walls around them, develop trust issues and start to feel comfortable with their pain because that is what they become used to. Even if they don't like it or want it, they attract similar or familiar situations and/or people in their reality that keep giving them similar experiences and in many cases, blame destiny for their circumstances, and stay ignorant to the fact that everyone's reality is their very own manifestation. Taking the accountability of our manifestation gives us the power to change it. How we see our parents or close associations treat each other, how loved, unloved, wanted, unwanted, accepted, detached we felt as a child, even what we watched on media between the ages of five and seven, all comes into play when we define life for ourselves subconsciously and start manifesting it at a very young age.

Without this awareness, people fall out of one situation or relationship as adults and get into another one only to find themselves in the same pattern or outcome that they desperately want to change but fail to do their pre requisite healing work that they must complete in order to manifest the life that they truly want, either because they don't want to accept that they need to heal or because they don't know the path to it and often their very own ego or self stands in the way of their acceptance or surrender to the change that they deeply desire.

Here is a fun fact, regardless of how perfect or not so perfect one's life has been, if they are on this planet, they have seen or experienced suffering at some level and if they have seen or known suffering, they must heal their emotions, mind, body and soul and not push their unhealed emotions under the rug. A focused and healed life is a life that is experienced fully in each moment. It is a life that is fearless, full of joy and gratitude. A life that is meaningful to oneself and others.

Once we understand and accept that sitting with ourself and healing our physical, emotional and/or mental body is what one needs, we unblock resources provided to us by the universe and several paths appear before us. Just like a child trying new classes to see what method of learning or area of interest is meant for him, we become children ready to explore spirituality. From this point on, we become hungry for knowledge and take on the new journey of the self, to the self and that is the game changer.

Exercise: Sit in silence and look through the experiences of your life as an outsider. Do you see a familiarity or a pattern in events, especially the unpleasant ones? What do you think this might be trying to teach you? (Some of the examples are self-love, self-respect, self-care, acceptance, forgiveness, humility, gratitude, appreciation, overcoming guilt or shame, humbleness- what is it that you lack?)

Power of Clarity

Acceptance of reality must be followed by time set-aside for reflection. We tend to get so entangled in our day-to-day life that we often forget the importance of giving attention to oneself, and the passing thoughts and emotions that are affecting our lives without us noticing it. Without spending the time alone, making self-reflections, we live life like we are dust carried through the wind of survival. It is favorable to the ego to stay in denial of reality and our own contribution to it, especially when the outcome isn't what we might have hoped for or when we experience a non-alignment of our wants to that of others around us. It is rather crucial to spend time alone to sit with ourself with complete honesty and do what is most important for actual well-being i.e., get clarity and take responsibility of our own actions.

Clarity is knowing what path our life has took us through, reasoning of why we had to take the path that we were led to and see the bigger picture to understand what is the purpose of it all and what are the lessons that we need to learn to make the shift. It is noticeable that when we learn our lessons, our life starts to change for the better but for that, we first need to be willing to make the changes within ourselves before they start manifesting in the world outside because this process of manifestation is inevitable. Just like the reflection in a mirror, we are afterall, what we attract.

We all know that change is vital for growth but what determines if the change will bring a positive outcome or a negative one is highly dependent upon how much time we devote in an honest conversation with ourself before attempting to have a conversation with others. Clarity brings understanding of our deep rooted emotions and helps us make the choices in life as knowledgeable, conscious beings with logic and abilities to judge, to sustain a humble approach of non-judgement towards the self and others, while maintaining balance between the heart and the mind, respecting the known and the unknown, keeping empathy of our own emotions, opinions and those of others, sustaining patience between reality and desired manifestation, and a deep understanding of the divine energy exchange.

Clarity is often clouded by our desires, specially the ones governed by deep emotions and uncontrollable passion of how we want our reality to shape. Manifestation is real and the power of our thought is strong therefore, we often attract what we fear if we lack clarity. Clarity cleanses our thoughts. It helps us see things for what they really are from a higher perspective. It helps us accept and forgive, learn and reform.. If confusion takes over, it becomes important to prioritize without attachment and find the ultimate balance between desires and needs. Once needs are met, desires can be fulfilled with ease of mind. Manifestation of what we want is accelerated, if we first appreciate and give our best to what we have.

Clarity is knowing what we want and what steps we must undertake to achieve our goals. It is in knowing when to follow the heart v/s mind and knowing that they have to be brought into balance or alignment. Clarity is looking sincerely at our contribution to our suffering. It's recognizing that the mind will create fear, obstacles and doubts to protect us – that is what our sympathetic nervous system is supposed to do but the heart and intuition must be trusted and fed to activate our parasympathetic nervous system to calm our fears down and create our desired reality. Clarity is making a decision that feels right to both, the heart and the mind regardless of the reasoning. It is important to remember that just because our mind thinks of a decision to be logical, it is not wise to ignore what the heart feels about it. In fact, if the heart doesn't feel great about something, it is probably not the path that our soul is guiding us towards.

Exercise: Sit with your eyes closed and ask your higher self to connect you to your truest desires. Try visualizing a healed life, happiness and everything that you would like to achieve in this lifetime. Do you see your purpose clearly?

Power of Intention

The third power to step into on the path of healing is the power of setting intentions. Intentions could be releasing held emotions that are long due to be released, or a promise to the self, to stay focused on our goals and purpose of life, while trusting the divine timing and the process. When we have clear intention, we send the message to the universe that "we are ready".. We are no more at a place of confusion, wanting one thing one day and changing our mind the next which in turn creates confusing circumstances and a life that we call a roller coaster- the one that throws and punches us when we least expect it. We blame our life and karma and call it destiny but it is in reality, us sending wrong signals to the universe. We blame the manifestations that our own mind creates because we do not take responsibility of it. When our intentions are clear, the universe aligns its resources to assist us in accomplishing our goals. When our intentions are set, we keep faith even in our low moments, knowing that every step is leading to the next, taking us to what we want and if we experience a setback in the process, it is after all a process and we have to let it happen without resistance and disappointments. We keep faith that it may be a much-needed change in the direction for something better to happen. While we are incapable of looking at the bigger picture from our naked eyes, we must understand that the universe is perhaps able to see it. We don't know the people we are about to meet, opportunities we are about to encounter and it is only when we reach a certain point that we look back and realize that all dots connect and it all makes sense.

There are traditions set in place by various cultures to set intentions. It is believable that if we perform a ceremony and write our intentions down in a beautiful way, it leaves a greater impact on our mind and we remember it more clearly versus sitting in meditation and going over them even though it serves the same purpose. One of the most popular rituals that is known to leave an impression on people is writing what you must release and let go, on a piece of paper and burn it on a full moon night. Similarly, writing what you want or must achieve on a new moon night is equally affective. As you burn the paper and see the smoke rise above, know that it is taking your message to the universe. It is crucial to remember that you can use such techniques or just simply meditate and allow your thoughts to become firm with intentions without performing any traditional rituals, the results you get by setting your intentions is equally proportionate to the level of faith you have in its manifestation and the divine timing.

The best intentions are those that exclude other outside influences and are limited to the person setting them. For example, setting an intention to be more open to love or releasing fears pertinent to commitment. Setting an intention to love yourself more or be more open to criticism to improve the self. Setting an intention to feel empowered and stand up for yourself when needed. Intentions help solidify short term goals and help us stay determined by believing in ourselves and the universe.

Exercise: Take two pieces of paper. On one paper, write down what you must release to clear the space for what you want and on the other paper, write down what you want for your life. Burn the first paper (preferably on a full moon but not needed) and as it burns, feel the relief of letting go. Burn the paper of your desired manifestation (preferably on a new moon but not needed) and as it burns, feel that the universe has heard your prayers.

Power of Thought

We pay attention to our actions, our words, our emotions and as we tame them, we often ignore the most powerful resource that we have and allow it to run like a wild horse – our thoughts.

It is important to feed our brain healthy just like we must feed our body the right nutrition. Our brain constantly adapts what we read and see, and just like a computer, it processes that information, forming our thoughts, beliefs, emotions, manifestations and ultimately our life as a whole. A negative thought cannot bring a positive outcome and it is important to realize that every single thought that we have manifests one way or another.

Just like when we want water, our brain instructs our hand to extend to the bottle of water, in reach, each of our thoughts, positive or negative form into planned or unplanned actions to make that thought our reality. Controlling our thoughts may be the most difficult step in spiritual expansion because we carry the baggage of conditioned beliefs. We understand that our actions build our reality, but totally ignore the fact that our thoughts create our actions, voluntary as well as involuntary, consciously and subconsciously, unknowingly and unknowingly.

It is also important to recognize that our brain works to create fear to protect us, often causing us to self-sabotage many things in our life that can turn out to be great if given a chance. For an example, if we burn our hand once, we are reminded of it every time we get close to a flame and if the burn was bad enough, we may not enjoy a candle light dinner like another individual who has fond memories of a bonfire, because our thoughts will take us back to that pain. To overcome the fears that our brain inflicts upon us, often before we make any major changes in life, like a new job or business, to relocate and start a new life, to trust once again in relationships, we must understand that the past is to teach lessons, brain is to alert us – but intuition is what we must follow and give our life another chance. Once we learn our lessons and apply them positively in any situation with an open heart, the outcome will be worth taking the risk and it will always take us to the next stage in life.

Changing our thought pattern takes committment. One of the best practices we can turn into a habit, is to be aware of our thoughts. It is the practice of mindfulness and being present. Keeping a check on ourselves perhaps, setting a reminder on our phone every hour for an affirmation that is positive like, 'this moment is special and it is all I have'. 'I am present', 'I am ready for happiness', etc. brings great results. Affirmations, when used regularly turn into beliefs. Just like a language coded in a computer, that's what our brain starts reacting to and we manifest our reality based on the instructions we give our brain through them.

Another great thing one can do to tame thought process is practice gratitude. Every morning and preferably also at night, we must go through the list of things that are working out well for us - thanking the universe for health, family, work, roof above our head, friends, career, love, everything that we can think of that we cherish in our life. Gratitude not only multiplies what we have but because it makes our thoughts positive, further impacting our emotions to be positive, we start attracting what we appreciate. Understanding that even our negative experiences will bring something positive in our life if we allow our shallow ego to break and humble ourself to learning, brings the change that we yearn.

Exercise: Write down five to ten things that you are grateful for. At any time, you feel that life is being unfair to you, go back to the list to bring yourself back into balance.

Power of Manifestation

Once the thought is turned into an emotion, we give birth to reality. We often underestimate the power within us to create our own life and settle for what we call destiny. We need to understand that we create our destiny on our own and we have the tools that we need to change it, if we desire so.

When we want something to happen in our life, we put a lot of effort in making it happen. We think of new ways to go after it, stress over it and in the worst-case scenario, get sad or depressed because what we want is not our current state of reality. This is because we miss the key - which is knowing, that our emotions are what directs our manifestations. We must shift our focus from 'what we want' to 'how we would feel once we have it'. Once we start feeling the emotion, the reality will follow and not the other way around. We must be happy and have gratitude for what we have, in order to attract more material wealth. We must give ourself the love and appreciation that we deserve before we attract someone else to value us. We must be lively in every moment to encounter experiences that make life a fun adventure.

To manifest what we desire, we first need to know what exactly do we want, how we will feel once we have it and then trust that it will happen as the universe shifts and things move to bring us in a place where we are ready to receive it. Manifestations may occur in a moment or it may take years for us to experience what we create. The timing depends on how well we manage or control our emotions through the process and how ready we are to receive our manifestation. Universe is like a parent to us. It knows that it is easy to take things for granted if we haven't learned our soul lessons. We need to have faith and not fall apart if our manifestation has not come to fruition as quickly as we would like it to manifest. Nothing holds more value than consistency to use this power. If we are given something before, we are ready for it, it is likely that we will destroy it just like a child who does not know better for his/her age or does not value or appreciate what is given to us at that moment because of distraction or simply because of the lack of understanding the misalignment between our ask and the desired outcome. For example, wanting someone to love us deeply is a great ask but asking it from a person who is incapable of providing us that love, for any reason, delays our manifestation. If we just focus on the emotion that we will feel, when we are loved, the universe will find us the best match who can give that love to us in the way we want it, but if we add a particular person to this dynamic, who is not ready or does not love the way we want to be loved or is simply still in the process of learning their own life lessons before they are able to manifest lasting love in their life, then we must understand that our manifestation may not feel the way that we want or may take ages or lifetimes because this particular person has their own path to follow, their own lessons that they may need to learn and two people have to be in alignment at the right time, space and reality to come together and that requires patience. While it is possible that two people who fall apart because of misalignment but keep manifesting each-other, can come together once again after learning their lessons through a separation, this kind of manifestation narrows the resources the universe can materialize for us in a scenario where our manifestation – which is being loved, is free of another individual. If we leave our manifestation for love open ended and focus on "how" love feels to us, the universe will find what's in our alignment, much faster. It may be with the person on our mind or someone we have never met who is best for our highest good. Similarly, if our desire is to pay a debt off or increase income, we must plant a seed and leave its fruition on the universe – an application to our dream job, rolling out a small business idea, writing a book, turning our art into profession and letting the universe take care of the rest. If our desire is to grow more spiritually, and be a better version of ourself, we must be open to ideas and receiving knowledge because the doors will open and a teacher will appear.

Just like any other area of spirituality, there are many paths one can explore in order to manifest. Use of water, redirection of sexual energy at the moment of orgasm when all our chakras our aligned, writing and burning rituals at new moon and visualization during meditation are some of the popular techniques that have proven to work for people that have entrusted their faith upon it. I encourage you to try the technique below with complete faith and leave the timing or exact result of manifestation upon the Universe. Who knows, you may receive more than you ask for.

Exercise: Put a glass of water in front of you. Take a small piece of paper and briefly right down what briefly write your desire and stick it on the glass. Hold the glass of water and sit with your eyes closed and visualize what you wrote and feel like it is happening. Recognize the emotion you feel as it happens. Now in an empty glass, pour this water slowly and feel your current reality is shifting and feel the emotion of your manifestation again. Now drink this water and know that it is about to happen. You may save the paper you stuck on the glass or discard it.

Power of Chakras

We are energy beings. Our energy or spiritual body that surrounds our physical body consists of layers – astral body, etheric body, celestial or emotional and, mental body that influence the vibration we radiate and vice-versa. Together, this energy field around a physical body or an object is called 'aura'. Aura can be of any color and each color represents emotional and physical health of its human. Invisible to naked eyes of those who are spiritually unawaken, our spiritual body is the home of our chakras (energy centers) that are formed while we are still in the womb, each one deriving its impressions from our pre-existing sub-conscious and unconscious reality that we have been carrying forward, and constantly forming via our surroundings as we age. Although, there are a total of 114 chakras in our body, the 7 major chakras are placed along the length of the spine. Each chakra varies in size and movement for each individual.

Shaped as a flower, each petal of a chakra is impacted by a certain energy or trait of the human behavior which overall determines the health of that chakra and furthermore, the physical body and our manifestations. Our surroundings make our belief system. Our belief system generates our traits and thoughts, that turn into actions, giving birth to our physical and emotional reality. As an example, root chakra has four petals. The bij mantra (chant) of each of these are – vam, sham, sha and sa. The petal with the sound vibration 'vam' tends to get blocked due to the sense of fear in an individual. Similarly, 'Sham' is blocked if a person lies, even if these lies are little and insignificant furthermore blocking the prana flow and movement of this chakra. If the root chakra is blocked, an individual suffers from body aches, intoxication and lack of peace.

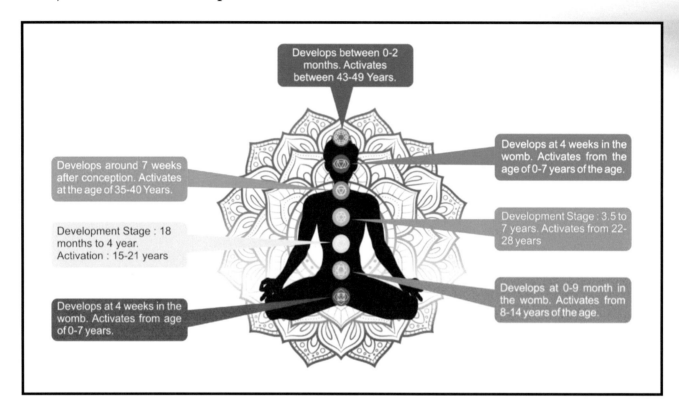

Chakras, when imbalanced, can be over active or underactive. To determine the right way to bring them into balance, it is vital to know its exact imbalanced state so we know what has to be given or taken away fragrances, crystals, etc.). There are various paths one can take to heal and balance chakras. There are specific yogasanas (yoga postures), meditation techniques, mudra (meditation with hand gestures), crystal healing, Cosmo/energy healing, etc., that have proven to activate, cleanse and balance one's energy body. According to Patanjali – the sage and author who gave yoga the attention it deserved; one must follow the eight limbs of yoga to attain the complete yogic state – the state of samadhi where we are equal to nothing. It's a state of total surrender that can only be achieved once the chakras are balanced. While in today's modern world, it may be harder for some people than others to follow all eight limbs of yoga and make it their lifestyle, whatever one can adapt makes a difference.

The eight limbs of yoga are the following:

Yamas – <u>Five Restraints</u> (Ahimsa- Non-Violence, Satya – Non-Lying, Asteya- Non-Stealing, Brahmacharya – Moderation, Right Use of Energy or Celibacy and, Aparigraha- Non-Attachment)

Niyamas – <u>Five Self-Disciplines</u> (Saucha – Cleanliness, Santosha – Contentment, Tapas – Discipline and Moderation, Svadhyaya – Spiritual Study and Isvara Pranidhana – Surrendering to the Divine)

Asana – <u>Physical Practice/Yoga</u>

Pranayama – <u>Breath Control</u>

Pratyahara – <u>Withdrawal of the Senses</u>

Dharana – <u>Concentration</u>

Dhyana – <u>Meditation</u>

Samadhi - <u>Bliss</u>

Exercise: See table 1.0 below to understand chakras and its functions. Based on the balanced and unbalanced characteristics listed in the table, determine which of your chakras need to heal.

Chakra	Color/ Day	Seed sound	Element	Essential Oils	Crystals	Associated Gland	Physiological System	Balanced Chakra	Imbalanced Chakra	Quality and Direction
Muladhar (Root Chakra) Number of Petals: 4	Red/ Saturday	Collective Sound: Lum Petal Sounds: Lum, Vum, Shum, Sha, Sum	Earth	Cedarwood, Clove, Rosemary, Rosewood, Thyme, Ginger	Black Tourmaline, Smokey Quartz, Red Jasper, Obsidian, Garnet, Hematite	Adrenal	Excretory System	Stability, Well Grounded, Prosperity, Confidence, Good Health	Urinary Disease, Kidney Disorder, Genital Disorders, Lower Back Problems, Cramps, Anxiety, Fear, Depression, Panic Attacks, Overthinking, Nightmares	Masculine Qualities Spins Clockwise in Males and Anti-Clockwise in Females.
Svadhishtana (Sacral) Number of Petals: 6	Orange/ Friday	Collective Sound: Vum Petal Sounds: Va, Ba, Ma, Bha, Ya, Ra, La	Water	Citronella, Fir, Lemon, Lime, Pine, Tea Tree	Chrysocolla, Jade, Clear Quartz	Adrenal	Reproductive System	Creativity, Movement, Procreation, Healthy Desires, Love for Pleasure, and Happy Relationships	Infertility, Tissue Disease, Genital Disorders, Lower Back Pain, Emotional Imbalances, Codependency, Addictive Behavior, Mood Swings, Feeling Guilt or Shame	Feminine Qualities Spins Clockwise in Females and Anti-Clockwise in Males
Manipura Number of Petals: 10	Yellow/ Tuesday	Collective Sound: Rum Petal Sounds: Daṁ, Dhaṁ, Naṁ, Taṁ, Thaṁ, Daaṁ, Dhaṁ, Naṁ, Paṁ, Phaṁ	Fire	Sandalwood, Myrrh, Atlas Cedarwood, Lemongrass, Lavender	Citrine, Amber, Topaz, and Yellow Gemstones	Pancreatic	Digestive System	Responsible, Reliable, Good Self-Esteem, Balanced Ego-Strength, Sense of Humor, Ability to Face Life Challenges	Digestive System Disorders, Diabetes, Low Immunity, Low Self Esteem, Addiction to Sedatives, Stubbornness, Victim Mentality, Power Struggles, Eating Disorders	Masculine Qualities Spins Clockwise in Males and Anti-Clockwise in Females

Anhata (Heart) Number of Petals: 12	Green/ Wednesday	Collective Sound: Yum Petal Sounds: Kaṁ, Khaṁ, Gaṁ, Ghaṁ, Naṁ, Caṁ, Chaṁ, Jaṁ, Jhaṁ, Naṁ, Taṁ, Thaṁ	Air	Jasmin, Lavender, Rose	Rose Quartz, Rhodochrosite, Aventurine, Jade, Prehnite, Amazonite, Malachite	Thymus	Circulatory System	Compassionate, Self-Loving, Peaceful, Balanced, Empathetic, Good Immune System	Heart Disease, Hypertension, Demanding, Clingy, Overly Sacrificing, Depression, Loneliness, Narcissism. Judgmental, Critical, Intolerant, Withdrawn	Feminine Qualities Spins Clockwise in Females and Anti-Clockwise in Males
Vishuddhi (Throat) Number of Petals: 16	Blue/ Thursday	Collective Sound: Hum Petal Sounds: Aṁ, Amṁ, Iṁ, Imṁ, Uṁ, Uumṁ, Rṁ, Rmṁ Lṁ, Lmṁ Eṁ, Aiṁ, Oṁ, Auṁ Aṁ, Aḥ	Ether	Oregano, Frankincense, Jasmine, Sage, Cypress, Peppermint, Eucalyptus, Chamomile	Turquoise, Sapphire, Aquamarine	Thyroid	Respiratory System	Loving/Clear Communication, Expressiveness, Good listening Skills, Good Sense of Direction	Bronchial Asthma, Lung Disorders, Thyroid, Goiter, Sarcasm, Fear of Public Speaking, Excessive Talking, Inability to listen, Loud/ Dominating Voice, Defensiveness	Masculine Qualities Spins Clockwise in Males and Anti-Clockwise in Females
Ajna (Third eye) Number of Petals: 2	Indigo/ Sunday	Collective Sound: Aum Petal Sounds: Hum, Shum	Mental/ Emotional body	Lavender, Lemon, Clary Sage, Juniper, Sweet Marjoram	Amethyst, Lapis Lazuli, Labradorite, Black Obsidian, Clear Quartz	Pineal	Nervous System	Strong Intuition, Clear Visions, Strong Imagination, Inspired, Accepting, Wisdom	Epilepsy, fainting, paralysis, Poor Concentration, Poor Vision, Hallucinations. Denials, Poor Memory, Lack of Imagination, Delusional, Obsessiveness, Nightmares, ADD/ADHD, Over Analytical	Feminine Qualities Spins Clockwise in Females and Anti-Clockwise in Males

Sahastra (Crown)	Violet/ Tuesday	Collective Sound Om Namah Shivay	Pure Conscious-ness	Sandalwood, Vetiver, Spikenard, Rose, Neroli, Pire Frankincense	Clear Quartz, Moonstone, Fluorite, White Agate, Howlite. Selenite, Amethyst	Pituitary	Central Nervous System	Open Mindedness, Broad Understanding, Inner Wisdom, Ability to Astral Travel, Channeling Spirits, Ability to Perceive, Mindfulness	Hormonal imbalances, Metabolic Syndromes, Spiritual Cynicism or Addiction, Greed, Trust Issues, Inability to Learn or Retain Information, Confusion	Neutral Qualities Spins Clockwise in Males and Anti-Clockwise in Females
Number of Petals: 1000										

Power of Meditation

Many people misunderstand meditation to be a form of disconnect. On the contrary, meditation helps connect – to the supreme, to one's higher self, to the universe, to the breath, to one's mind, to the nature or whatever helps one's mind get centered so deeply that everything else fades away naturally. Guided meditation is a great way to start experiencing the stillness one can feel during the practice. There is no single perfect or right way to meditate, the perfect method is the one that works for an individual and that can be different for everyone. Yogis spend majority of their time meditating and hence seem extraordinarily peaceful and balanced however, for most people who are entangled between work and wordily responsibility, blocking that kind of time is impractical however, there are practices like mindfulness that one can start with, to begin being aware and to adapt a new, peaceful lifestyle and then slowly commit to five, ten or up to ninety or more minutes a day, based on the time they are able to hold focus and their availability to sit in silence, experiencing meditative peacefulness.

Meditation has various physiological and psychological benefits. It doesn't only improve our power of focus and concentration, but also improves memory retention, relieves stress, boosts our immune system and health, and rejuvenates us. Below are a few techniques one can try for meditation but the deeper you look, the more ways you will find and create for yourself. It is not the method that matters, it's the result.

*Please note, although practicing meditation has great benefits at any given time of the day or night, it is most affective between 3:40 to 4:30 in the morning because this is the time when our prana (life-flow) revolves around our heart chakra that opens and receives energies. If meditation is practiced at this time, it amplifies its benefits.

Mindfulness: This is one of the easiest techniques of meditation that can be done several times a day to bring yourself to the present moment. Sit in silence for a few minutes and bring your attention to the subtle sounds you hear. It could be of the fan, air, birds, or just your breath. The objective is to be present. You can then start practicing mindfulness to bring yourself to the present moment any given time of the day while doing whatever you may be doing. Mindfulness is not just a meditation technique, it's a habit you form.

Chakra Meditation: Sit in silence and start putting your focus on each chakra starting from the base/root chakra moving one by one upwards to the crown. If you are able to visualize colors then imagine the color of each chakra surrounding the area of that chakra illuminating its shade brightly extending and slowly surrounding you and your environment. If you remember the bij chant (can be found in chakra table on page 15) of the chakra, you may choose to chant it while you work at each chakra. Spend a few minutes focusing on each chakra and then another minute in the end affirming that all your chakras are activated, balanced and healed.

Affirmations: Sit in silence and find your affirmation. Affirmations can be small sentences in present tense stating what you want like you already have it. For example, "I am healed, I am enough, I am loved, I am prosperous, I attract abundance, etc.". Feel the emotion as you affirm to yourself.

Ho'oponopono: This is an ancient Hawaiian meditation technique that has proven to be beneficial for forgiveness and anxiety. Close your eyes and take a few deep breaths, connect with your heart chakra by putting a hand on your heart and find any emotion that is bothering you and repeat, "I am sorry, please forgive me, I love you, thank you". You can use this to forgive yourself for hurting your inner child by not letting go intense emotions or forgive others for not knowing enough or, unintentionally or intentionally hurting you. Over time, this meditation helps release emotions and helps you start with a clean slate.

Breathing: Controlling your breath is one of the most popular meditation techniques among yogis. There are various techniques collectively known as 'Pranayama' that guide the prana – the life-giving force, to flow in the body and spread oxygen for overall improvement in health. One can use simple deep breaths to start, or count to take a deep breath i.e. inhale to the count of four, hold for the count of seven and release at the count of eight. Counting helps keep our focus centered. As you get comfortable and are able to hold the breath longer with ease, you can increase the count based on your ability.

Chanting: 'Mantras' are sound waves with frequencies, each having a certain effect on the body and mind. Repeating the same frequency or sound over and over is believed to create a vibration that has a healing affect. It also helps bring mind to the center. For finding the right mantra/chant one must be certain of the purpose behind one's meditation practice.

Third Eye Activation: Typically used to evoke one's psychic abilities or the sixth sense, third eye meditation requires one to massage the center of the brow area for a few seconds then focus on this point and about two inches inward at the pineal gland with eyes closed, eyeballs rolling upwards. This meditation may cause a little strain in the beginning on the forehead as the third eye starts to flick open but if done regularly, over time, one develops the ability to see the past, present and future. It is recommended that such practices should be done only if you are in contact with a guru or teacher who can guide you in the right direction because through activating this chakra, you may open doors to the other dimensions in the universe.

Exercise: Pick any of the meditation techniques listed above and practice for at least ten minutes but preferably for 22 minutes a day for at least 21 days.

Power of Yoga

Yoga is a Sanskrit word that literally means 'yolk' or 'coming together'. Yogasana – exercise postures are a form of workout that is not only advantageous for the body but also for the mind and soul. It is a workout technique that helps release stored stress, anxiety and trauma in the body and helps activate chakras to bring a human to his/her full potential in the present. Yoga, for its complete benefits is practiced with intention and meditation to program the mind. There are different kinds of yoga practices designed for people who have different goals e.g.: Hatha (Practiced at a moderate pace and has aspects of all other forms of yoga), Kundalini (devotional/spiritual yoga), Vinyasa (flow-based yoga generally practiced on a fast pace), Restorative (helps people recover from injuries), Yin (deep stretches), Pranayama (breathing techniques), etc.

While all yoga practices have their own benefits and work as different paths to the same destination which is good physical and mental health, some practices are beneficial for a specific result than others. For example, breathing techniques like 'anulom vilom', also known as alternate breathing works great for 'nadi shodhan' which means cleaning of the air/nasal passages which in turn improves the flow of prana in the body. Similarly, yin yoga, with the deep hip stretches helps release deep rooted emotions in the body with its twisting techniques and lubricates our joints.

What a lot of people don't realize is that yoga works beyond the mat. Since it is interpreted as a form of workout, its psychological benefits are often overlooked or underestimated. While most workout techniques, if done correctly and in moderation, help release endorphins and keep our body moving, yoga helps heal the energy body along with the physical and brings every element within our body into balance.

A yogi who sits in meditation to attain spiritual powers can do very little without embracing the practice of asanas (postures).

Exercise: Pick any of the yoga styles based on your current ability to work out and practice 60 minutes of asana either in a yoga studio or online. Try to be consistent for at least 3 weeks to feel a difference.

Power of Mudras

It was between 4th and 9th century that eating with cutlery started becoming a fashion. In many ancient cultures, an incredible amount of appreciation is given to the benefits of eating with hands. It is believed that each of our fingertips sustain the power of one of the five elements present in the body (Earth, Water, Space, Fire and, Air), control points for the three body types (Vata, Pita and Kapha), points for planetary influence that impacts our physical body and astrological affects in a birth chart, nerves connected to every part of the body and chakras (energy centers). The technique of putting fingertips together and reciting the appropriate chant with it, has helped many people achieve a state of samadhi or fulfil their worldly desires through sidhi (manifestation power obtained by specific meditation techniques performed for a certain time). This method balances chakras, elements and the effects of planetary influence in an individual.

Mudras or hand gestures, used during meditation have been believed to be beneficial for thousands of years in many cultures. We can especially find many ancient Chinese, Buddhist and Hindu depictions of God and Yogis with their hands and fingertips placed a certain way in a meditative pose.

Each mudra has a different benefit that we will discuss in the next few pages. There is a mudra technique for almost every physical and emotional ailment that you can think of.

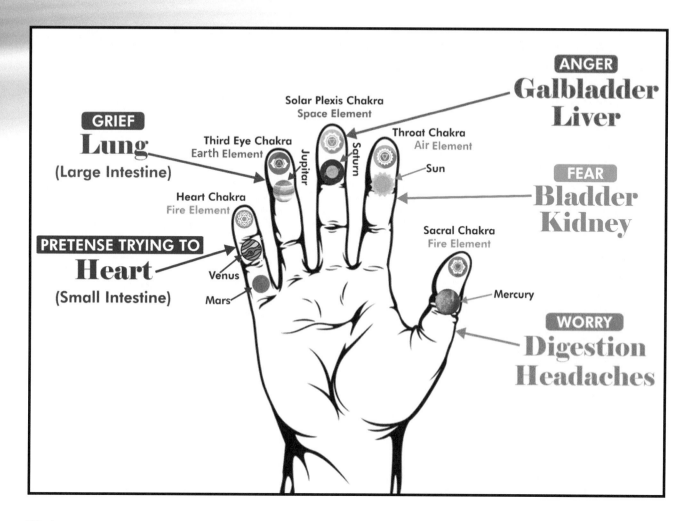

Mudras have two particular techniques. Fingertips touching one another or one fingertip touching the mounts (base of our fingers) on our palms. If our palm is open, facing upwards and one fingertip touches another, we invoke masculine energy within us. With this method, our breath and focus reaches the gyan chakra (third-eye). When we chant audibly in this method, we attain knowledge. On the other hand, if we allow our fingertips to touch the mounts at the bottom of our fingertips so our hands are partially closed and we chant silently in our head, we invoke the feminine energy within us and attain powers.

Exercise: The table below highlights a few basic mudras, the technique and the benefits. Try some of them for 22-45 minutes for 21 days and notice the differences you feel within yourself.

Mudra	Method	Chant	Sense	Prana Flow	Helps Resolve Problems
Gyan Mudra Open	Tip of the Index Finger Joining the Tip of the Thumb	Om/ Om Shiva Shivay Om Namah Shivay/ Om Lum Vum Rum Yum Hum Om Namah Shivay	Sight	Third Eye Chakra	Heart Related Problems, Activates Third Eye-Psychic Powers, Eyesight, Oxygen, Diabetes, Insomnia, Blood Pressure, Activates Sushumna nadi, Helps Weight Loss, Resolves Problems in Family
Vayu Mudra Closed	Tip of the Index Finger Touching the Mount of the Thumb and the Thumb Touching the Back of the Middle Finger	Om	Sight	Throat or heart	Gastritis, Heart, Paralysis, Shaking Hands, Injuries, Sprain, Chest Pain, Builds Immunity Against Cold and Cough, Helps Weight Loss, Bone Cracks or Neck Disorders
Akash Mudra	Tip of the Middle Finger Touching the Tip of the Thumb	Vum	Hearing & Taste	Throat or heart	Liver Related Problems, Activates Clairaudience, Blood pressure, Throat Related Problems
Shunya Mudra	Tip of the Middle Finger Touching the Mount of the Thumb and the Tip of the Thumb Touching the Back of the Middle Finger	Om	Hearing	Throat	Clairaudient Psychic Power, Vertigo, Ear Disorders, Numbness, Cures Bi-Dosha or Tri-Dosha
Prithvi Mudra	Tip of the Ring Finger Touching the Tip of the Thumb	Lum/ Om Lum	Smell	Tip of the Nose	Digestion, Balances Pitta Dosha, Promotes Hair Growth, Helps Gain Weight, Reduces Heat in the Body, Boosts Spiritual Stability, Balances Kapha Dosha

Surya Mudra	Tip of the Ring Finger Touching the Mount of the Thumb and the Tip of the Thumb Touching the Back of the Middle Finger	Kleem Baushath	N/A	Different for Everyone	Helps Weight Loss; Throat, Ear, Nose Related Problems, Face Stiffness, Helps Financial Issues, Removes Negativity, Pitta Dosha
Jal Mudra	Tip of the Little Finger Touching the Tip of the Thumb	Vum	Touch, Taste	Throat	Bladder, Kidney, Lungs, Inflammation, Stress, Lower Back Problems, Improves Power/Influence of Speech, Activates Throat Chakra, Resolves Reproductive Issues, Helps Relationships, Rejuvenates
Vipreet Jal Mudra	Tip of the Little Finger Touching the Mount of the Thumb and the Tip of the Thumb Touching the Back of Little Finger.	Om Lum Vum Rum Yum Hum Om Namah Shivay	Touch	Different for Everyone	Inflammation
Vyan Mudra	Tips of the Index and Middle Fingers Joining the Tip of the Thumb	Vum (Sacral Chakra); Vum Swadhishthan Jagre Vum Om Phat	N/A	Sacral to Crown Chakra	Kidney Related Problems, Improves Blood Circulation, Gives Energy, Reduction of Sweat, Thirst and Hunger, Improves Mood Swings
Vishnu Mudra	Tip of the Index and Middle Fingers Joining the Mount of the Thumb	Om Lum Vum Rum Yum Hum Om Namah Shivay	N/A	Different for Everyone	Reduces Stress. Helps Headaches, Cures Asthma, Allergies, Snoring, Blood Pressure, Calms Mind, Helps Anxiety, Diabetes

Apan Open	Tips of the Middle Finger and Ring Finger Touching the Tip of the Thumb	Lum (Root Chakra)/ Om Lum Param Tattvai Gum Om Phat	N/A	Root to Solar Plexis Chakra	Activates Root and Sacral Chakra, Relieves Joint Pain, Helps Cancer Cells
Vipreet Apan Mudra	Tips of the Middle Finger and Ring Finger Touching the Mount of the Thumb and the Tip of the Thumb Touching the Back of the Two Fingers	N/A	N/A	Different for Everyone	Weight Loss, Balances Protein and Calcium in Body, *(Middle finger helps heal fatty liver and Ring Finger heals Pitta Dosha)*
Pran Mudra	Tips of the Little and Ring Fingers Joining the Tip of the Thumb	Yum (Heart Chakra)/ Om Yum Anahat Chakra Jagre Jagre Shreem Om Phat	N/A	Heart to the Tip of the Nose	Activates Left and Right-Side Chakras of the Body, Diabetes, Heart Related Problems, Overall Health/Immunity, Increases Power of Attraction
Udan Mudra	Tips of Index, Middle and Ring Finger Joining the Tip of the Thumb	Hum (Throat Chakra)/ Om Hrom Joom Sah	Heart	Throat to Crown Chakra	Thyroid, Brain, Boosts Memory and Mental Clarity, Enhances Creativity
Saman Mudra	Tips of All Four Fingers Joining the Tip of the Thumb	Rum (Solar Plexis Chakra)	N/A	Solar Plexis to Heart Chakra	Aches and Pain, Balances Metabolism, Improves Liver Functions, Balances Dosha, Increases Appetite, Helps Hypertension, Liver Functions
	Tip of the Thumb on the Mount of Little Finger	N/A Focus on Breath	N/A	Different for Everyone	Anxiety
	Apan mudra on left hand and vyan mudra on right hand	Om Lum Vum Om	N/A	Different for Everyone	Low/High Blood Pressure, Brings Positivity in Life

	Udaan Mudra on Right Hand and Apaan Mudra on the Left	Om Lum Vum Rum Yum Hum Om	N/A	Different for Everyone	Thyroid
	Tip of the Thumb Touching the Mount of the Middle Finger	N/A Focus on Breath	N/A	Different for Everyone	Ears, Nose and Throat Related Problems
	Tip of the Thumb on the Mount of Index Finger	N/A Focus on Breath	N/A	Different for Everyone	Toothache, Skin Problems

Power of Ayurveda

Developed over 5000 years ago in India, Ayurveda is a practice of holistic healing through natural Medicine, healthy lifestyle and food. This Sanskrit term, if literally translated means, life science. It is an all-natural medicine system that is plant and nutrients based.

The study of Ayurveda suggests that there are three body characteristics known as 'dosha' in a human body. The three doshas named as Vata (wind), Pitta (fire) and Kapha (earth and water) are present in every human with one of these working as a dominant force over the other two. This dominant dosha determines a particular individual's body type which further explains what areas in the physical body are harmed due to access of these elements and what the body lacks to bring these into balance. This determination helps build a plan of what nutrients or food a body needs and what has to be reduced in order to neutralize the effect of the dominant dosha and increase the efficiency of the weak ones. For example, a body that has excessive Pitta or fire element must reduce the food intake that generate excessive heat in the body therefore the diet for this body type should include more cooling foods. It is interesting to realize that the food we eat doesn't only affect our physical body but also our moods, emotions and energy.

Vata, the element of air, has the ability to balance the other two doshas along with it. Vata dosha is found to be cold, dry quick, moving, changeable, lively and enthusiastic. People with prominent Vata usually have a lean body and an energy that draws others towards them. Vatas are emotional, sensitive and empathetic. They easily pick up on what others are feeling. When in conflict, Vatas try to find a solution, peacefully. When imbalanced, such people can experience physical/bodily issues like constipation, hypertension, weakness, arthritis, restlessness and other stomach or digestion related problems. Vata pacifying foods are soft & mushy, sweet, salty and sour. Some examples are, whole grains, root vegetables, nuts, healthy fats, natural sweeteners and fruits.

Consisting of fire and water together, *Pitta* dosha controls digestion, metabolism, and energy production. People with high levels of Pitta have a fiery nature. They are usually of medium size and weight. They may have bright red hair, baldness or thin hair. They have excellent digestion, which sometimes leads them to believe they can eat anything. They sleep soundly for short periods of time and have a strong sex drive. When in balance, Pittas have a lustrous complexion, perfect digestion, abundant energy, and a strong appetite. When out of balance, Pittas may suffer from skin rashes, burning sensations, peptic ulcers, excessive body heat, heartburn, and indigestion. Pittas have a strong concentration power and they are good decision-makers, teachers, and speakers. They are precise, sharp-witted, direct, and often outspoken. Out-of-balance pittas can be short-tempered and argumentative. Pittas should work on managing their time and not skip meals to avoid being reactive. Cooling foods such as cucumbers, melons and sweet fruits are beneficial to pittas. Dairy can also help balance the heat of Pitta. Sour, fermented products such as ygurt, sour cream, and cheese should be avoided as sour tastes aggravate Pitta.

Kapha governs the structure of the body, it holds the cells together and forms the muscle, fat and bones. Kaphas have a strong build and high stamina, large and soft eyes, smooth - radiant skin and, thick hair. Those who are predominantly Kapha sleep soundly and have regular digestion. Excessive Kapha can cause weight gain, fluid retention, and allergies, excessive sleep, asthma, diabetes, and depression. Kaphas are naturally calm, thoughtful, and loving. They have an inherent ability to enjoy life and are comfortable with routine. When in balance, Kaphas are strong, loyal, patient, steady, and supportive. People with an excess of Kapha tend to hold on to things, jobs, and relationships long after they are no longer nourishing or necessary. Excessive Kapha in the mind manifests as resistance to change and stubbornness. In the face of stress, Kaphas try to ignore the problem and run away from dealing with it. Kaphas should avoid dairy and most sweeteners except honey. They should consider drinking hot ginger tea with meals to help with digestion and eat beans, lighter fruits, vegetables and pungent spices. Kaphas should avoid nuts, seeds, oats, rice and wheat.

Another interesting fact that helps work with balancing of the three doshas is that they all have a certain time of the day that they are more active. Pitta is active during 12 pm-8 pm, Vata is active between 8 pm and 5 am and, Kapha is active between 5 am to 12 pm. Once determined, which one of our dosha is overactive or underactive, one should consider eating the specific dosha friendly food (when possible, meditate – mudra or perform yogasana or pranayama in the specific dosha hours for its complete benefit.

The other benefit of Ayurveda as discussed above is its medicinal study. Based on Ayurveda research of years (going back to the ancient times), certain plants and grains have medicinal uses. For example, Neem plant or Azadirachta indica is great for the teeth, turmeric has anti-inflammatory properties, the combination of yogurt and rice, if eaten for twenty-one days in a row, improves the quality of one's skin and helps people with prolonged sinus related pains, garlic purifies vayu (air) in the body, onion (if taken in moderation) balances pitta dosha and green pumpkin removes toxins from the body. Also, to increase immunity, drinking a glass of green pumpkin juice with a little ginger juice and black pepper is extremely helpful.

There is a remedy for every physical problem one may encounter in this science of natural medicine. Ayurveda has proven to be beneficial to bring people at their correct body weight and recovering from illnesses. For this to happen, one must drink at least three liters of water every day.

Exercise: Take a free dosha test on www.Aatmayog.co and discover your body type. Read about what food is good or bad for your dosha and make modifications in your current diet accordingly.

Power of Energy Healing

Everything and every being is energy. The physics of gravitational pull of an object going up in the air to fall back on the surface, seen through spiritual eyes is called Karma or in simple terms, 'what goes around comes around'. Our intention has energy that is more powerful than one can imagine. A person who cooks food with loving thoughts and energy prepares a magical meal that is emotionally healthy for the people consuming it versus a person cooking it with negative emotion of just for having to do so. People who consume the food cooked with happiness will unknowingly develop happy emotions unlike people who end up with a meal that was cooked by an individual with a negative state of mind. Similarly, because water is known to absorb energies the most, even a covered glass of water, absorbs the emotions of people around it. When consumed, it leaves either a positive and healing impact or a negative and deteriorating impact on people. Several manifestation practitioners believe in the use of water to strengthen their practice because of how it absorbs energy.

As humans, we constantly stay busy in our daily grind, interacting with people, finding ourselves in pleasant and unpleasant situations, keeping expectations, creating emotions in ourselves and leaving an impact on others unknowingly. We do not realize how every single moment of our life has energetically impacted our existence and what we manifest due to it. Energy healing is a process of cleansing all that no longer serves us and brings us in a state of mind that is like a clean slate, ready to start a fresh life like a child. Once cleansed, we have the power to restart and recreate our life the way we want it.

There are various kinds of energy healings like Angel Therapy where angels are called upon to heal, Reiki which is an energy channel that the practitioner is initiated with, and is able to open within themselves and then pass the energy healing to the patient, Pranic Healing which invites 'prana' or life-giving force from the universe to heal the patient through visualization, sound healing that uses sound frequencies to activate healing vibration in the brain and body cells and Cosmo Healing, which is the only healing technique that uses 840 frequencies available in the Universe/Cosmo accessed through cosmic channels to heal and balance the energies in the human body. It cleanses our chakras, meridians, organs, energy or biofield. This healing is so powerful that it is capable of starting a fire with the heat that radiates out of a healer's hand. A Cosmo healer has to be not just initiated but educated in the energy healing field and knowledgeable of physiology and energy body to use this healing appropriately.

Energy healing has not only proven to heal the emotions, lifestyle and relationships of people with themselves and others but also chronic illnesses and diseases. Even though, it can be slow, it is an effective way of healing, that requires the patient to be open to receiving the healing by keeping the belief in the process, just like the placebo effect in modern medicine. The time taken to heal through Cosmo energy is different for each individual depending upon the condition of the person, the age, openness to healing and willingness to change. Although, Cosmo energy can be felt and its results can be seen during and right after a strong session, it is recommended to at least get six to ten sessions of healing to feel a lasting affect (in some severe cases, the number of sessions is increased), each session lasting anywhere between 20-45 minutes.

Exercise: Sit and put your hands a few centimeters apart like you are holding an imaginary ball. Close your eyes and invite the prana or lifegiving force to come between your hands. Once you start to feel the tingling on your palms, gently pull your hands closer and/or apart to feel the prana or energy. Give this ball of energy an instruction to heal a certain emotion or pain that you are carrying and then send this ball to the required area to heal. Sit with this healing a little longer and feel the relief.

Power of Surrender

There is nothing better one can do for themselves than to try their best and then let go. Surrendering does not imply non-doing. It means that one is at their highest potential at any given moment to situations and people around them but has no expectations of any return. The intention behind an individual doing something for another must stem from the good in themselves and what one does for their own good must originate from a mindful thought of what is right for the highest good of everyone involved and not just themselves, based on their understanding.

Surrendering implies being humble and accepting to not just one's own but also to other's point of view. It implies trusting the divine timing and keeping the faith that, because one step leads to the other, whatever is happening is taking one to where they are supposed to go.

According to Buddhist teachings, there are five virtues, i.e., wisdom, kindness, patience, generosity and compassion. If one lives life making these virtues a part of their lifestyle and true nature, it eliminates the harsh emotions of vices such as anger, hatred, greed or envy, ultimately improving one's quality of life, creating joyful experiences in every moment. For a person to attain this wisdom, they need to be honest with themselves about where their beliefs are, and only then they can commit to being mindful to change their thought patterns. Someone who is not open to change is not open to growth or spiritual expansion and ultimately cannot reach the state of bliss that a human can experience – the state that often hides behind one's veil of ego.

Humans generally have a tendency to consciously or subconsciously control – people, outcomes and circumstances. It is not always with ill intentions, sometimes we simply feel responsible for people around us or situations we are in, specially of our children and loved ones. We may think we are protecting them by not allowing them to have the space to make their own decisions but because we think our opinion is the right one, we often unknowingly sabotage or delay their growth. Needless to say there are some instances that require us to intervene or guide people for safety but that choice must be made carefully. One must guide where they can but leave the decision on the individual unless it's a situation that is life threatening. The best we can do is be honest about everything to everyone. In our relationship or circumstances, we are constantly involved with other people who have their own free will, their own lessons that they need to learn in this lifetime, their own path that they need to take and the only power that we have is the power to surrender to reality and then either accept and make peace with it while giving our best and support their healing through other avenues because they are extremely important to us or take on a new path if the situation is toxic and keep faith in Universe's bigger plans that leads us to a good place. We forget that fighting to control or change situations will only bring negative emotion to the situation and negativity only attracts negativity. It is sometimes best to give people space to breathe and support them to figure life out on their own and allow things to fall into place in its own time.

Gautam Buddha teaches us, there are three solutions to every problem: accept it, change it, or leave it. If you can't accept it, change it. If you can't change it, leave it.

Exercise: Think of any situation that did not work the way you wanted it to. Perform an accountability exercise by being honest with yourself without any judgements. What is the role that you played in your suffering? What could you have done differently to alter or avoid that state or situation? Send yourself love, acceptance and forgiveness and then pass on the same emotions energetically, to the related situation or people.

Power of Aatmayog

Aatmayog or 'oneness of soul', is a healing practice of yoga that is developed after years of research on healing different aspects of life through the practice of yoga, meditation, Cosmo healing, Emotional Freedom Technique (EFT), Neuro-Linguistic Programming (NLP) and others, integrated as a transformational technique.

The practice of Aatmayog is to heal one's emotions and remove deep rooted blockages so a human radiates abundance and attains happiness by bringing different aspects of spiritual healing together as one practice.

It is developed so people have access to one technique that brings many healing avenues together, instead of having to go different routes to try different things to see what brings people the most benefit. Since most people do not have time to analyze life and find out what state they are at, physically, mentally and emotionally and what is the spiritual cause of it, Aatmayoga's intake process not only finds out an individual's current state but can also help create an individualized plan to take them to the next stage of expansion and abundance.

One session of Aatmayog practice covers asana, mudra, meditation, chakra balancing and energy healing altered to one's needs.

Other than private sessions, corporate workshops and retreats, Aatmayog also offers group sessions for general wellbeing.

Aatmayog retreats and practice locations can be found at: www.aatmayog.co

Printed in the United States
by Baker & Taylor Publisher Services